P9-EKX-320

A CAMBRIDGE TOPIC BOOK

The Industrial Revolution Begins

Christine Vialls

Published in cooperation with Cambridge University Press
Lerner Publications Company, Minneapolis

Editors' Note: In preparing this edition of *The Cambridge Topic Books* for publication, the editors have made only a few minor changes in the original material. In some isolated cases, British spelling and usage were altered in order to avoid possible confusion for our readers. Whenever necessary, information was added to clarify references to people, places, and events in British history. An index was also provided in each volume.

LIBRARY OF CONGRESS CATALOGING IN PUBLICATION DATA

Vialls, Christine.
  The industrial revolution begins.

  (A Cambridge topic book)
  Originally published as: Coalbrookdale and the iron
revolution. Cambridge; New York: Cambridge University Press, 1980.
  Includes index.
  Summary: An account of Coalbrookdale in western England's
Severn Valley, scene of some of the earliest and most interesting
developments of the Industrial Revolution. Also discusses the
work of iron manufacturers like Alexander Darby, an industrial
pioneer.
  1. Iron industry and trade—England—Coalbrookdale—
History. 2. Coalbrookdale (Salop)—Industries—History.
[1. Industry—History. 2. Iron industry and trade—England—History.
3. Coalbrookdale (Salop)—Industries—History] I. Title.
HD9521.8.C8V5 1982   338.4′76691′0942456   81-13714
ISBN 0-8225-1223-8 (lib. bdg.)   AACR2

This edition first published 1982 by Lerner Publications Company
by permission of Cambridge University Press.

Original edition copyright © 1980 by Cambridge University Press
as part of *The Cambridge Introduction to the History of Mankind: Topic Book*
under the title *Coalbrookdale and the Iron Revolution.*

International Standard Book Number: 0-8225-1223-8
Library of Congress Catalog Card Number: 81-13714

Manufactured in the United States of America

This edition is available exclusively from:
Lerner Publications Company, 241 First Avenue North, Minneapolis, Minnesota 55401

1 2 3 4 5 6 7 8 9 10 86 85 84 83 82

Contents

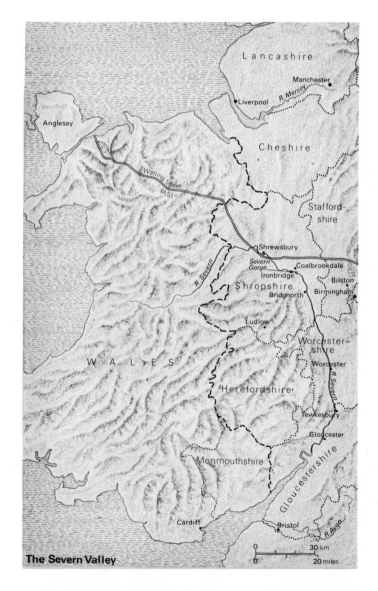

The Severn Valley

1 The Severn Gorge in 1700

On New Year's Day, 1781, traffic crossed the River Severn by the new iron bridge for the first time. Even before it was finished people had been coming from all over Britain to see it. Now, two hundred years later, thousands of people still come from all over the world to see this bridge of iron. To understand why it aroused so much interest in the late eighteenth century and why it is, today, preserved as a symbol – perhaps the most important single symbol – of the early Industrial Revolution, we need to think back to the beginning of that century, to 1700.

The Iron Bridge crosses the river near the middle of the Severn Gorge. This is a narrow valley with the River Severn lying about 100 metres (330 feet) below the surrounding countryside. The steep sides of the valley are heavily wooded and the river is deep and treacherous. It can rise to flood point very quickly and its swift currents were hazardous to the many craft which once used the river.

In 1711, there were only about eleven and a half thousand people living in the whole of the east Shropshire coalfield. About half of this area is shown on the map opposite. Some of these people were farmers, and others were employed in the local industries. Most of the farms were small; farmers usually kept cows, and sold cheese made from the milk, as well as growing some crops. Oxen were still used for ploughing in some parts.

By the beginning of the eighteenth century the district round the gorge already had a variety of industries. Below the soil lay coal and ironstone. As early as 1250 the monks of

Buildwas Abbey were mining coal and by the time Henry VIII dissolved the monasteries there were several small ironworks which were run by the monks. By 1700 iron and coal provided the two most important industries in the district. As well as making finished articles in iron, the local smiths produced many bars of iron for sale to the nail-makers who lived in Worcestershire and South Staffordshire. Iron was also sold to chain-makers and, of course, to blacksmiths for shoeing horses and for making tools such as scythes and knives.

There were also a few other small industries in the gorge area. In the village of Jackfield mugs and dishes were made of the local clay, and some of the poorer local clay was probably made into bricks for house-building. Very fine white clay was used to make the long white churchwarden pipes which men liked to smoke. Some of the rocks in the area were limestone

Seventeenth-century wrought-iron tools.

blacksmith's tool

wood axe

pruning knife

sickle

branding iron

left: *This map drawn by Robert Baugh shows the area round Coalbrookdale and the Severn Gorge, about 1808. It shows clearly not only the nature of the countryside, but also eighteenth-century developments, which made the area famous.*

below: *Rose Cottages in Coalbrookdale. These wood-framed cottages were probably built in 1642 and are the oldest surviving houses in the dale.*

below: *Rush lights like this were made by stripping the green skin from reeds and dipping the pith into hot fat. This holder could also be used to hold a small candle. It dates from the eighteenth century and was probably made by a village black-smith.*

below: *Rose Cottages in Coalbrookdale. These wood-framed cottages were probably built in 1642 and are the oldest surviving houses in the dale.*

below: *Rush lights like this were made by stripping the green skin from reeds and dipping the pith into hot fat. This holder could also be used to hold a small candle. It dates from the eighteenth century and was probably made by a village black-smith.*

and these were mined or quarried near the gorge. The iron-workers needed limestone to help them to produce good iron. Lime was made by burning limestone in kilns. It was used for building and as a fertiliser by the farmers in the area.

Even the mines were small. Probably only four or five men were employed in each one, possibly with the menfolk of one family working together. A tunnel driven into the side of a hill was the most usual type of mineworking since shafts driven straight down into the ground were more difficult to make and were also much more likely to flood.

The houses near the gorge were scattered round the district in ones and twos. For instance, in Coalbrookdale, a long valley running at right angles to the gorge, there were only about five houses, where the workmen for an ironworks and two forges lived. The little community was very isolated. Records show

that the workers were not paid in money but in bacon, meat, butter and cheese. Apart from the iron industry, most work was done by small groups of people in their own living-rooms or in small workshops attached to their houses.

Most cottagers would have had some land of their own and often kept a pig and some hens. The better-off cottagers might even have owned a cow. Their main food would have been bread; not bread as we know it today, but dark rough bread made of rye grown on the local farms instead of wheat. They would probably not have grown potatoes which were still regarded with suspicion in most areas. Young children were given milk to drink, but older children and adults drank ale which was malt beer made without hops. Coffee and tea were known in London by this time, but no poor workers could possibly afford to drink them, even if they had heard of them.

News travelled very slowly to country districts. There were few news sheets and most of the country folk were unable to read. Travel was rare except for the wealthy who had horses to ride and they normally only travelled in the summer months because of the muddy state of the roads. Poor people could usually go only as far as their legs could carry them.

Almost everything had to be done by hand. Clothes, curtains, sheets and blankets were woven by hand out of yarn which had been hand-spun. Furniture was hand-made; bread was made in small ovens heated by wood fires and candles were made by the housewife out of mutton dripping.

For the ordinary people of 1700, wood was their most important commodity. The framework of their houses was made with it, their carts were made of it and it was used to build the ferries which carried them across the river. Large river boats were also made of wood.

Electricity, gas, steam power and the petrol engine were not even imagined. The only forms of power available in 1700 were wind, water and animal power. Most villages would have a mill, turned by water or wind. This was often owned by a big landowner and all the cottagers who grew their own rye would take it to the mill to be ground into the rough flour they used to make bread.

right: *A sketch of a packman offering ribbons to a cottager. The picture is from Pyne's* Microcosm, *published in 1807, but sights like this must have been very common all over the country for many centuries.*

Roads, rivers and waggonways

When the Romans were in Britain they had built excellent roads all over the country. But, after they left, the British did not keep the roads in repair. Worse than this, many people took the stone paving from the old Roman roads because it was good building material for houses or barns. Once these stones were removed, the roads began to break up. Local people were supposed to keep the roads usable, but often they made very little effort.

In many places the Romans had built bridges. Many, especially in sparsely populated districts, were not repaired or replaced, and through the years they had collapsed leaving rough muddy fords which no cart could pass over. Any wheeled traffic had to find a way round through the fields on either side of the old road. In 1700 it was so difficult for carts to pass along many roads that most goods were carried by pack-horses; even breakable things, like pottery cups and jugs, would have to be packed into the baskets on the horses' sides. And, of course, the packman who visited all the houses and cottages trying to sell his ribbons, laces, buttons and thread was so called because he carried all he had to sell in a pack, slung either on his own back or on a packhorse.

One great Roman road, Watling Street, passed within a few kilometres of the Severn Gorge. This was not in good repair, and the small roads linking it with the gorge were very bad indeed, so bad in fact that almost all goods travelled to and from the gorge by water. The River Severn was one of the busiest rivers in Europe. Well over 160 km (100 miles) of river was suitable for boats, which meant that the people in many inland areas of western England and eastern Wales were able to make use of the river.

A number of the men who lived in the gorge were boat owners who earned their living by carrying coal up the river to Shrewsbury and to parts of mid-Wales, or down river to Worcester and Tewkesbury. They used sailing boats, and it was, of course, often difficult for them to sail up-river against the stream and so on awkward stretches the boats were pulled up-stream by gangs of six or eight men. This was hard work: the men would be bent double, often with their hands on the ground as they strained to move the boat against the flow of the river. To make things even more difficult for them, there was no proper path for them to struggle along, so that they had to pick their way along the banks, as they hauled on the ropes.

Before about 1600, most of the coal would have been carried to the river from the mines in baskets slung over the backs of packhorses. One horse would only be able to carry about 200 kg (nearly 4 cwt), so long trains of these animals had to walk along the muddy tracks, often with the reins of one horse plaited into the tail of the horse in front, to enable one man to lead a line of as many as twenty horses. This was a very slow way of moving coal. It was also very expensive because so many horses had to be kept and fed.

Soon after the year 1600 a new method of moving coal began to be used in Shropshire. Wooden waggonways were built from the mines down to the River Severn. Small wooden waggons ran on large clumsy wooden wheels with a wooden flange on one side of each wheel to stop the truck from sliding

A modern wheelwright repairing an old cartwheel, using methods and tools which were used in the eighteenth century.

off the rails. The rails themselves were also made of wood. The tracks of the waggonways were built on long slopes so that the waggons ran down to the river under their own weight. The empty waggons were probably pulled back up to the mine by horses.

These wooden waggonways had a great advantage over the ordinary roads. As we have seen, many roads were little more than mud tracks which regularly became impassable in bad weather. The wheels of a cart would sink deep into the mud until the body of the cart was at ground level. This made it impossible for even a team of eight horses to move the cart. Imagine the difference when wooden rails were laid down. Now the full weight of the cart, resting on its four wheels was distributed over two lengths of wooden track; even in bad weather it would keep on working.

By the year 1700 most of the mines would have had a waggonway to take out the coal. However, the ordinary roads were still so bad that most goods were carried by water.

2 Cast iron

Early ironworking

Archaeologists tell us that it is at least four thousand years since man discovered iron. But during most of those years its use was greatly restricted by the problems attached to preparing it from the ore. At first man had to heat his iron ore in small charcoal fires. This changed the ore into a lump of iron. The process was slow as only very small amounts of iron could be made at one time. So in those early days iron was in effect a precious metal.

We think that these early ironworkers must have noticed that on a windy day their fire burnt more brightly and the iron ore seemed to change more quickly. What is certain is that men began to use an artificial wind; they used bellows to make the fire hotter. These were probably made from animal skins stretched over a frame made of tree branches. There would be two bellows so that as one was blowing the other could be filling with air. This made the work faster. Often the two sets of bellows were worked by a man actually standing on them in turn. A great deal of air – or blast, as the iron-makers call it – was needed to keep the fire hot enough. It took several hours' work to change the iron ore, and the lump of iron produced from an average furnace would weigh only about 2 kg (4 or 5 lb). This would be hammered into such things as helmets, scythes, swords and nails.

One catastrophe could overtake these early ironworkers. If the process was not managed properly the iron would turn from a spongy lump into a liquid state and could not be hammered into shape. Then the ironworkers could do nothing with it. All the iron in the furnace had to be thrown away and their hours of work had produced nothing. We know that this sometimes happened, because when archaeologists have excavated old furnaces, they have sometimes found lumps of iron which have obviously been melted to this liquid state and have then been thrown onto a rubbish heap.

In parts of Northern Ghana, until about 1950, workable iron was made in clay furnaces. In 1973 some villagers built one to show archaeologists how it was done. Above you can see the bottle-shaped furnace and men working two pairs of bellows. A skin with a hole in is tied over the top of each bowl of the bellows. When the man lifts the skin air enters the bowl through the hole; when he presses down on the skin to pump air into the furnace he closes the hole with his wrist. Below, the furnace has just been broken open, to get out the iron.

Archaeologists have also discovered that in China iron-workers found a way of turning this molten or liquid iron into statuettes as early as AD 500. Molten bronze had been cast into moulds earlier than this but the melting point of bronze is much lower than that of iron. It was probably not until about AD 500 that men were able to raise the temperature of their furnaces to a point when iron would melt other than by accident.

In the fifteenth century, ironworkers in Europe began to develop their own techniques for using molten iron. The men made moulds in the ground, probably out of sand, and filled them with the liquid metal. The iron would solidify in the sand mould and when hard would take up the shape of the mould. This method, which we call casting, was used for making such things as cannons and firebacks.

From that time onwards, men in Europe began to value this cast iron. New types of furnace were built with stone walls lined with special clays which could withstand the heat of the melting iron. The man-powered bellows were not powerful enough to produce the draught needed to heat these new, larger furnaces. But mechanically minded men soon learned to harness water power to help them. A waterwheel turned a studded shaft which in turn pressed down on the bellows, forcing air into the bottom of the fire, which then burnt more fiercely. This helped to turn the ore into liquid iron.

The iron ore which men dug out of the ground was never pure. It always had other elements, such as sulphur, phosphorus and manganese, mixed with it and, as it was dug out of the ground, there was always a certain amount of clay or sand and dirt. To remove the impurities, the ironworkers added some limestone to the furnace. This became liquid in the heat and the impurities in the ore combined with it to make what we now call slag. As this liquid was lighter than liquid iron, the slag floated on top of the iron and was run off from the higher part of the furnace. For many years this slag was considered a waste product, and huge slag heaps developed near ironworks.

After the slag had been removed the molten iron was run off from the bottom of the furnace into sand beds which had been shaped into moulds. These moulds usually consisted of a long channel with many small short channels running at right angles to it. It was an exciting and rather frightening sight to see the white-hot river of iron running along the main channel and gradually flowing into all the smaller ones. Seeing these small moulds lying in neat rows at right angles to the main river of metal, men were reminded of a litter of piglets being suckled by the sow and so the iron straight from the blast furnace came to be called pig iron. This process of making cast or pig iron from iron ore in a blast furnace is called reducing the ore or smelting.

This diagram shows how a waterwheel was used to power the bellows which provided the air blast needed to smelt the iron ore in the furnace.

below: *The inside of a foundry near the Severn Gorge in 1788. The men are standing beside the white-hot river of pig iron as it fills up the channels in the sand. The crane would have been used to lift pigs and other iron castings when they were cool.*

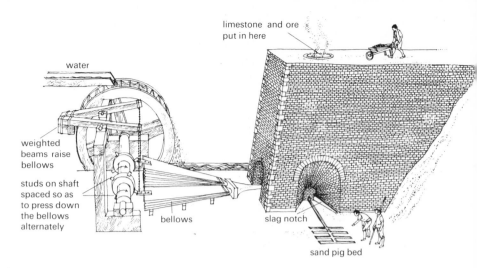

water

limestone and ore put in here

weighted beams raise bellows

studs on shaft spaced so as to press down the bellows alternately

bellows

slag notch

sand pig bed

right: *Sticks ready to be covered with turf and soil, to be made into charcoal. The fire will be lit through the hole at the top of the heap.*

far right: *A charcoal heap which has just been lit. The wood pile underneath the turf and soil will smoulder until it is reduced to pure carbon.*

Smelting with charcoal

Ironworkers had found that charcoal was the only fuel that could be used in blast furnaces. But it had a great disadvantage. A vast quantity was needed and it was difficult to obtain. Charcoal was made by building a heap of wood and covering the heap with turf and soil. The bottom of the heap was then set alight and the amount of air admitted was controlled very carefully so that the wood never burst into flame. As the heap smouldered the wood was partially consumed by the heat so that all the gases and moisture were driven off and the hard fibrous part of the timber was blackened and dried, leaving the pure carbon which the ironmaster needed in order to change his ore into iron. After about five days, when no more gases rose from the heap, the charcoal burner broke it open.

By the beginning of the seventeenth century there were about eighty-five blast furnaces working in Britain, all consuming large quantities of charcoal. There was never enough charcoal, and most blast furnaces had to close down for part of each year (sometimes for nearly half a year at a time) while fresh supplies of charcoal were accumulated. For once the

furnace was 'in blast' – was lit and working – it would be kept working day and night, seven days a week, month after month until the charcoal was used up or the water supply which powered the bellows dwindled.

The supply of charcoal was limited by the availability of wood for the charcoal burner to use. As we have already seen, wood was used for many purposes in the years before 1700. Whole forests were cut down to build the great wooden ships for the Navy and those needed to carry goods and passengers. The shortage of wood forced the ironmasters of Cumberland to ship their iron ore across the Solway Firth into Scotland where wood was more readily available.

A great deal of the iron needed at that time was used by blacksmiths or else as bar iron for making nails. The blacksmith could not use cast iron from the blast furnaces until it had been reheated in a charcoal hearth to remove the excess carbon. This hearth was rather like that used by a modern blacksmith. The oxygen in the air blown into the hearth removed the excess carbon from the iron by combining with it, and thus turned the pig iron into wrought iron. So here again were men needing large supplies of charcoal. No wonder iron was in short supply.

It was obvious that the output of iron would always remain limited until some other fuel could be used to smelt the ore. The ironmasters must often have wished that they could smelt with coal – especially as coal and iron ore are often found together. But coal contains large quantities of sulphur. This combines very easily with the iron during smelting. Unfortunately, iron with a high sulphur content is very brittle while hot. A blacksmith trying to forge anything from it will be quite unable to shape the iron; it will crumble and break under his hammer. Many people tried to solve this problem and some claimed to have been successful.

In the first half of the seventeenth century, Dud Dudley, the illegitimate son of Lord Dudley, claimed to have made iron using coal from the Dudley mines. But there is no evidence that he really did solve the problem; he himself admitted that he had only been able to produce usable iron on a few occasions.

Abraham Darby

This was the situation in the iron industry in 1708 when a man named Abraham Darby leased the small charcoal blast furnace at Coalbrookdale. He was thirty-two years old and had been born near Dudley, not far from where Dud Dudley had carried out his experiments in smelting with coal. Darby's father was a locksmith and nail-maker, and the whole family were Quakers – members of the Society of Friends. Young Abraham served his apprenticeship in Birmingham, which by then had a large Quaker community and was therefore a safe place at a time when Quakers were often persecuted for their religious beliefs. His master was another Quaker, a maker of malt mills for the brewing trade, and here Abraham learned to make machinery. Malt is made by drying grains of barley over coke fires. Because ale was the usual drink of the ordinary people, this trade offered a secure livelihood for a young man. It was also a trade needing skill in metalwork and no doubt young Abraham had learned much about metalwork from his father.

After his apprenticeship was completed Abraham married

Cooking pots cast by Abraham Darby when he first moved to Coalbrookdale. Many of the large pots were made for boiling sugar cane and can still be found in some parts of the West Indies.

and moved to Bristol, another town with a large Quaker community. Here he set up in business for himself as a malt-mill maker, but we know that before long he was making brass castings and later began to make cast-iron cooking pots. It was these pots which were his first products when he moved to Coalbrookdale. In the years that followed, the firm he founded exported them to many parts of the world.

Abraham Darby's first job when he took over the Coal-brookdale works was to re-build the furnace. We cannot be sure how long there had been a furnace on the site, but the date 1638, which can still be seen on the beam above the hearth, is probably the date when it was built. The firm's accounts for 1709 show that Darby was buying coal suitable for making into coke in the early months of that year. Coke was made by partially burning heaps of coal in the open air. All the natural gases were driven off by the heat, eventually leaving a heap of almost pure carbon. Abraham Darby must often have seen coke being made by the maltsters when he was making machinery for them.

As an ironmaster he would know the problems caused by the shortage of charcoal and he possibly knew about the experiments that Dud Dudley had carried out near his own home town. At some time Darby must have begun to recognise the similarity between coke and charcoal. In both cases

the fuel which, in its natural state, contained impurities was subjected to long periods of slow heat which drove off the unwanted gases and left a fuel consisting of nearly pure carbon. Perhaps it was when he saw this similarity that he decided to move to Coalbrookdale so that he would have his own blast furnace where he could carry out experiments using coke to smelt iron ore.

Smelting with coke

Before very long Darby was using iron from his coke-fired furnace to cast his cooking pots and many other small things such as kettles and smoothing irons. It is difficult for us to get an exact picture of what happened in Coalbrookdale during the first few years of Darby's occupation. (Perhaps we ought rather to be surprised at how much we do know about what happened well over 250 years ago.) But from the account books of the business, many of which still exist, and from stories written down by his descendants and by other people living in the dale, we can piece together a great deal of the story.

One thing is quite certain – Abraham Darby had not solved all the problems of coke smelting. The iron he produced in his coke-burning blast furnace was only suitable for making castings. From the accounts we know that he was still buying charcoal-smelted iron for use by the blacksmiths in his forge.

But he had taken the first, and most difficult, step towards freeing the iron-smelting industry from the tyranny of charcoal.

Abraham Darby does not seem to have tried to keep secret his new method of smelting with coke instead of charcoal. Neither did he go out of his way to publicise it. So far as we know, it was some time before other ironmasters tried to copy him, and when they did it seems almost certain that none of them was very successful. One reason for this may have been because they were using different coal. The coal which Abraham Darby would have used in Coalbrookdale had a very low sulphur content and this may have had a direct bearing on his initial success. In the eighteenth century there was a considerable amount of interest in chemistry so it is possible that Darby knew about the low sulphur content when he decided to carry out his experiments in that part of the country. Or it may just have been a fortunate accident which provided him with suitable coal. Whichever it was, his work brought about this important development in the technology of the iron industry which led to the period of growth in Britain which we now call the Industrial Revolution.

Over the next forty years some other ironmasters changed to smelting with coke. But, having solved the problem of fuel supply, they were now faced with a new problem: when they were using charcoal, their blast furnaces had had to close down regularly while they accumulated new supplies of fuel. Now that they were freed from this necessity, they found that they were faced with another difficulty: this was the unreliability of the power employed to work their bellows. The flow of water which drove their mill-wheels could be interrupted. Previously a drought had not mattered too much; they had had to close at some time during the year. Now, using coke as fuel, no such stoppage was necessary. A drought or a frost became a very unwelcome event, but they had no alternative to water power to work their blowing machinery.

3   Steam power

Engines for pumping

While Abraham Darby was carrying out his experiments in Coalbrookdale, Thomas Newcomen, an ironmonger, was conducting very different experiments in his home town of Dartmouth in Devon. Newcomen was almost certainly a skilled worker in such metals as lead, tin, copper and brass. He probably got a great deal of his trade by travelling round Devon and Cornwall collecting orders for small agricultural implements and for machine parts from outlying farms and from the tin mines.

During these journeys Newcomen must often have heard about the problems of the mine owners, the greatest of which was the water which flooded so many of the mineworkings. This was true of mines in many parts of the country, including the coalfields of the Midlands.

For many years horse gins had been used to lift water from the mines. As the horse walked round, the rope would be wound on a drum, so pulling the bucket slowly up out of the mine. This was quite an effective way of removing small amounts of water from the mineworkings, but, as seams of coal near the surface were worked out, miners had to go deeper for their minerals and the problem of water became much more serious. Mines often became totally unworkable, miners were put out of work and mine owners went bankrupt.

The need for a much more powerful method of pumping water must have been evident to Thomas Newcomen. His solution to the problem was to invent a pump powered by steam.

As early as the first century AD, Hero of Alexandria experimented with steam, but all he managed to make was a scientific toy. Since then there had been many other experiments involving steam. On occasions men had managed to lift small quantities of water using steam power, and a robust but slow steam pump was invented before 1700 by Thomas Savery, another Devon man. However, no one had managed to make a pump really adequate for use in the mines, until the ironmonger of Dartmouth perfected his engine.

A horse gin being used to lift baskets of coal out of a small mine, from a sketch made in 1805. On the far right you can see the two small wheels over which the cables pass to raise and lower the baskets. Men are unloading baskets of coal as they come up from the mine and the one in the foreground is breaking up large lumps of coal with a pick. A gin for raising water from mines would have been similar to this one.

right: *A Newcomen-type atmospheric engine built in 1795
at Elsecar, South Yorkshire; it was kept working until 1923
and is the only Newcomen engine in Britain still on its
original site. The wooden beam was replaced by a cast-iron
one in 1836–7. Every stroke of the engine lifted 227 litres
(50 gallons) of water out of the mine and it worked at
6 to 8 strokes a minute.*

right: *A piston from a
Newcomen engine. It is
about 60 cm (24 in.) in
diameter and measures
95 cm (37 in.) to where it
was joined to the chain
from the great beam (see
the picture opposite).
The rope wound round
the piston helped it to fit
tightly against the uneven
sides of the cylinder. The
pieces of iron on top of
the rope are weights to
hold it in position.*

Newcomen's first engine was built for a coalmine near
Dudley Castle only about 32 km (20 miles) from Coalbrookdale. This was in 1712, by which time Abraham Darby was
smelting iron ore with coke. At first sight it seems strange that
Newcomen's first steam pump should have been built in the
Midlands instead of in the West Country. But coal was plenti-
ful in the Midlands and there is no local coal in Devon and
Cornwall. Newcomen engines used a great deal of fuel to heat
the water in the boiler and one has to remember the difficulties
of shipping coal to the Cornish tin mines.

Seven years after the first Newcomen engine was built,
another Newcomen engine was working at Madeley near
Coalbrookdale. We do not know where this engine was made,
but it is quite possible that some of the parts were made at
Coalbrookdale. The records of the firm show that they were
making steam engine parts by 1718 but as the earlier records
are lost we cannot find out when they began making them.

In those days Newcomen would not have made an engine at
Dartmouth and then sold it to the mine at Madeley. Transport
was so difficult over muddy roads, with only horses to pull the
loads, that this would have been impossible. Instead, he would
have given the company instructions on how to build an engine
and they would have arranged for all the parts to be made.
Newcomen probably went to the mine himself to help them to
erect the engine and possibly the Madeley people managed to
get an engineer from the Dudley engine to help them to make
sure that their engine was working properly. This was a
difficult job because there were few men in the world who
understood such engines. (Remember that the first engine had
only been built seven years earlier.) On occasions they must
have had to follow out Newcomen's instructions without really
knowing what they were doing.

Although the pumping engines were used mostly on the
coalfield it was not only the mine owners who realised that
they might get help from the new steam pumps. In 1735 there

The ENGINE for Raising Water by Fire

Sutton Nicholls delin. et sculp. 1725.

Drawing of a Newcomen engine, dated 1725. It was published with a detailed explanation of how all the lettered parts worked, but even without this it gives a good idea of how the engine was used.

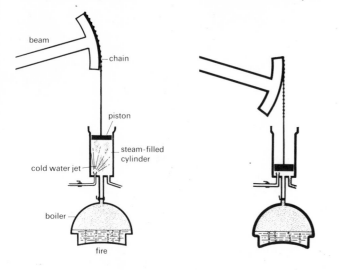

Newcomen engine: *piston at the top of the cylinder.*

Newcomen engine: *piston at the bottom of the cylinder.*

beam

chain

piston

steam-filled cylinder

cold water jet

boiler

fire

was a very low rainfall and the Coalbrookdale Company was getting short of water to drive their waterwheel. They decided to use a horse gin to lift the water from below the waterwheel back to the top again. In this way the same water could be used over and over again. The idea was so successful that they soon decided to build a steam engine to do the work.

Anyone who has left a kettle boiling in the kitchen will know that a very small quantity of water can soon fill a room with steam. It is this capacity for steam to expand until it fills every available space which has been behind all the experiments in steam power.

Perhaps the most noticeable feature of the Newcomen engine to anyone seeing it for the first time was the great beam. This was a huge balk of timber which could rock up and down like a grotesque see-saw. To one end of the beam were attached the pump rods which descended into the mine shaft, and below the opposite end of the beam were the working parts of the Newcomen engine.

The engine consisted basically of a cylinder with a moving piston inside it attached by a chain to the great beam above. Before the working stroke of the engine, the weight of the pump rods on the opposite end of the beam would have pulled the piston to the top of the cylinder, leaving a space below it. Steam was made to flow into this space. Then a jet of cold

water was fed into the steam-filled cylinder, making the hot steam turn back into quite a small quantity of water. This left a partial vacuum under the piston. The pressure of the atmosphere above the piston was now much greater than the pressure in the cylinder, and so drove the piston down to the bottom of the cylinder. The downward movement of the piston was the working stroke of the engine since it caused the other end of the beam to rise, so working the pump. As soon as more steam was let into the cylinder, the vacuum was released and the weight of the pump rods moved the piston to the top of the cylinder again, ready for the next stroke of the engine. Because the piston is actually worked by atmospheric pressure, experts prefer to call this an atmospheric engine rather than a steam engine.

A Swedish engineer who lived in England from 1716 to 1726 wrote a description of a Newcomen engine. He tells us that the pump rods lifted about twelve times a minute and that on each stroke the engine lifted 40 litres (nearly 9 gallons) of water out of the mine.

Separate condensers and tight cylinders

The Newcomen engine was inefficient, because the cylinder was first filled with steam and then cooled again by the water jet which turned the steam back into water. It then had to be heated up again for the next stroke of the engine. This was obviously a very wasteful use of heat energy and time.

The man who solved this problem was James Watt, a mathematical instrument maker in Glasgow. In 1764 Watt had been asked to repair a model of a Newcomen engine for a professor at Glasgow University. He quickly mastered how the atmospheric engine worked and realised that if he could find a way of keeping the cylinder hot and yet at the same time condense the steam, the engine's efficiency would be greatly improved. Then, in May 1765, he hit upon the idea of con-

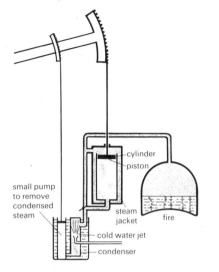

Before John Wilkinson died he had a tall cast-iron pillar made to be his own monument, but the wording, which was added after his death was not exactly what he himself had written.

densing the steam in a second vessel, which he called a condenser. Once the cylinder was full of steam, the steam was allowed by a valve to escape into the condenser where it was turned back into water. This enabled the cylinder to stay hot all the time and so the engine could work much faster, do more work and use less fuel. Watt went on to design engines where the piston was actually worked by the steam, not by the atmosphere: these were true steam engines.

– In 1768 Watt went to London to patent his invention of a separate condenser. On the way home he called on Matthew Boulton, then a well-known manufacturer of metal goods in the Midlands. The two men took an immediate liking to each other and in 1775, after more experimenting, Watt went into partnership with Boulton and moved to Birmingham.

One other problem had to be solved before the steam engine could become really efficient. This was the making of the cylinder. If the piston was to be a steam-tight fit in the cylinder, the inside of the cylinder had to be smooth and circular. Matthew Boulton suggested that they should approach an ironmaster named John Wilkinson, who owned the Bradley Ironworks near Bilston, Staffordshire, and an iron foundry at Willey, just above the Severn Gorge. Wilkinson was a great character. He had enormous enthusiasm for iron, and, perhaps more than any other man, pioneered its use for

many new purposes. When he told people that he was making an iron canal boat, they laughed and reminded him that iron would not float like wood. They nicknamed him Iron Mad Wilkinson and when the iron boat actually did float they suspected him of black magic.

He was a clever inventor and never afraid of going against authority. When there was a shortage of copper coin and the Royal Mint could not produce enough, Wilkinson had his own halfpenny (half an old penny) coin struck, with his head on the obverse side. At one time he even had his own silver coin struck and was only stopped by the Government from issuing his own paper money.

Matthew Boulton knew that Wilkinson had invented a new

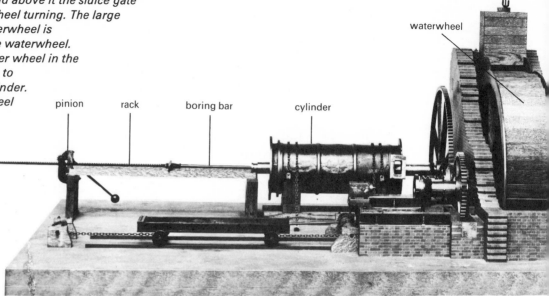

A model of John Wilkinson's cylinder-boring machine. On the right is the waterwheel and above it the sluice gate which was opened to start the wheel turning. The large gear wheel on the left of the waterwheel is mounted on the same axle as the waterwheel. This can be connected to a smaller wheel in the foreground which turns the lathe to make the circular ends of the cylinder.

Also mounted on the waterwheel axle is the long bar holding the cutting tool. The hollow cylinder which is to be bored is chained down on heavy blocks so that it cannot move. The heavy bar on which the cutter is mounted is supported on the left of the cylinder. The cutter was moved along inside the cylinder by means of the rack and pinion.

machine for boring cannon. Before this was invented cannon were usually cast hollow. But it was almost impossible to cast the bore of a cannon round enough and smooth enough. They had to be cut to shape after casting by being moved forward slowly against a rotating cutting tool. This method certainly shaped the bore so that at any point the barrel was round in section, but it was not necessarily straight, as the cutting tool tended to follow any irregularities in the cast bore.

John Wilkinson decided to cast his cannon solid. He then mounted his cutting head on a very strong and rigid bar. But instead of rotating the cutting head, he rotated the cannon itself. As the cutting head began to hollow out the bore, the cannon could be moved towards it very slowly by means of a screw thread.

Matthew Boulton saw that this type of machine might well be used to bore out the cylinder for James Watt's engine. However, Wilkinson realised that, unlike a cannon, a cylinder could be made open at both ends and so he designed a special cylinder-boring machine. In this the cutting head was the moving part, but, because of the open ends, it could be mounted on a solid bar which passed right through the cylin-

der and could be supported at each end. This prevented the cutting head from following any defects in the original casting.

James Watt was delighted with the results that this machine produced. After this he insisted that all his engines should have cylinders made by John Wilkinson. He was so certain of their quality that he was able to promise his clients that even a very large cylinder 'would not be further from absolute truth than the thickness of a thin sixpence in the worst part'. These new cylinders were an outstanding improvement on the ones used by Thomas Newcomen.

John Wilkinson was equally pleased with James Watt's engines. The second Watt engine was built at Wilkinson's works at New Willey in 1776. Wilkinson had tried to use a Newcomen atmospheric engine to pump the bellows in his blast furnace, but he had found that its stroke was too uneven to keep the blast going smoothly. However, the Watt engine was regular enough to work the bellows steadily. Before this, steam power had been used only to pump water to keep the waterwheel turning, a method which still had to be used to power the cylinder-boring machine.

Matthew Boulton was also using a steam engine to drive a

A halfpenny token coin minted in 1792 by John Wilkinson. One side shows a man holding a red-hot piece of iron on an anvil with a long-handled pair of tongs, while the heavy hammer is about to fall. On the other side is John Wilkinson's head.

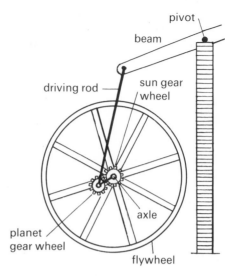

Sun and planet device. *The driving rod was moved up and down by the steam engine on the other end of the beam. This made the outer (planet) gear wheel travel round and turn the inner (sun) gear wheel, which turned the axle and thus worked the machinery.*

waterwheel in his own works and realised that what was needed was a steam engine which would drive machinery, such as the cylinder-boring machine, directly through a shaft or axle. He persuaded Watt to try to make his engine rotative.

Engines for turning wheels

A crank mechanism had been used for many years on foot lathes, converting the up-and-down movement of the foot pedal into the rotary movement needed for the lathe. James Watt could have used this principle in his steam engine but it had already been used by a man named Pickard to make a Newcomen-type engine rotative. Pickard had patented his idea and so James Watt decided to use a different method. He invented what is called the sun and planet mechanism in which a toothed gear wheel, fixed to the axle to be turned, is meshed with a similar gear wheel on the end of the rod from the engine. The up-and-down motion of the engine rod causes the second gear to travel round the first in the manner of a planet circling the sun. The sun and planet was not such a neat piece of mechanism as the crank, but Watt was not prepared to fight Pickard over the patent.

One of the characteristics of a rotative engine is its flywheel. This very heavy wheel keeps turning continuously while the

engine is working. Because of its great weight, it helps to even out any irregularities in the motion of the engine. This is very important, as many machines have to be kept running smoothly and continuously.

In 1788 John Wilkinson began to use a Watt engine to power his cylinder- and cannon-boring machines and this new use of steam soon spread. The introduction of steam power to turn rotary machinery had a profound effect on many industries, particularly in the textile mills which were appearing in parts of northern England. If a textile machine hesitated slightly, it would break the threads, but the new smooth-running steam engines drove the machines without jerking. Once factory owners were supplied with steam power they no longer needed to build their factories beside swift-running streams in remote valleys. Although they still needed water to cool the condensers of their Watt engines, they could now use mill ponds or the more slowly running rivers in the flat valley bottoms, where supplies of raw materials and labour were easier to obtain, and from where it was less difficult to despatch finished goods.

By the end of the eighteenth century big industrial towns were growing rapidly, and large numbers of agricultural workers were moving from the countryside into towns such as Manchester and Liverpool, Birmingham and Leeds.

4 Wrought iron

Abraham Darby solved the major problems of smelting iron ore with coke to make cast iron as early as 1709, though it was forty years before this process became common in the iron industry as a whole. Coke was easier to obtain and cheaper than charcoal, so ironmasters all over Britain now chose coke instead of charcoal as the fuel for their blast furnaces. But charcoal was still needed to produce wrought iron for the blacksmiths, and for rolling into sheets and rods. Pig iron contains more carbon than wrought iron. At that time the usual method of removing the excess carbon was to re-heat pig iron in a charcoal fire while blowing air across it. As the iron began to heat in the fire, the carbon combined with the oxygen in the air. The workers would stir the soft iron until enough carbon had been removed and they were left with wrought iron.

Once Abraham Darby had successfully used coke to smelt iron ore, many workers in the industry must have thought of ways of trying to use coke to convert pig iron into wrought iron. Records show that in 1766 two brothers working at Coalbrookdale took out a patent for using coke to turn pig iron into wrought iron. The patent says that they used a special furnace called a reverberatory furnace, and it seems to have been fairly successful. But it used a great deal of pig iron

above: The Menai suspension bridge built by Telford in 1825 which joins the island Anglesey to the mainland. The bridge was made largely of wrought iron and is suspended above the water by means of wrought-iron bars and chains.

compared with the amount of wrought iron that it made and so proved too expensive to use.

Seventeen years later another Coalbrookdale man, Peter Onions, also took out a patent for using coal as the fuel to produce wrought iron. But at about the same time, in 1784, a Hampshire man patented a method which proved so successful that the Coalbrookdale experiments were abandoned. The Hampshire man was Henry Cort. He also used a reverberatory furnace. By his method, the pig iron was heated by the flames from a coal fire, but the furnace was so built that the iron and coal were never in contact. This prevented any of the sulphur in the coal from entering the iron and making it brittle. Once the cast iron in the furnace had melted, it was stirred with an iron bar to bring all the iron into contact as quickly as possible with the current of air drawn through the furnace by the fire. The carbon in the iron then combined with the oxygen in the air, leaving wrought iron. The man who stirred the iron was known as the puddler and the process was called puddling.

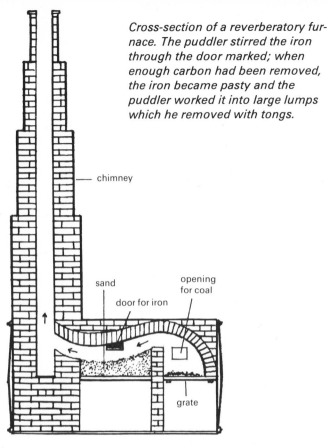

chimney

sand

door for iron

opening for coal

grate

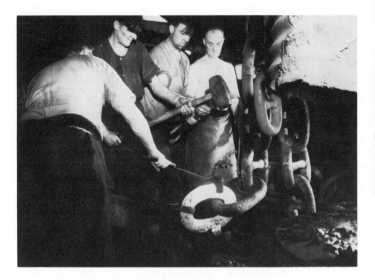

below: *The two hammer men are waiting ready to strike as a red-hot link is fitted onto a chain. Hand-forged wrought-iron chains continued to be made in Shropshire for many years.*

Cort's technique was soon adopted by ironmasters throughout Britain.

Henry Cort also made another great contribution to the iron industry. For many years red-hot wrought iron had been passed between two rollers, which the ironworkers called rolls, to press it out into sheets of iron. Henry Cort found that by cutting grooves in his rollers, he could make rods of different shapes and sizes according to the type of groove he made.

Henry Cort's method of making wrought iron was very similar to the two techniques first used at Coalbrookdale, and he was not the first man to use grooved rollers. His genius was that he made both his inventions work successfully. As time went by Cort's methods were modified and improved by other men in the iron industry. As more wrought iron became available, industry as a whole began to rely on it more and more. In 1740 less than twenty thousand tonnes of pig iron were made in Britain, but in 1840 the amount had risen to nearly one and a half million tonnes. Most of this was turned into wrought iron.

Because of the new techniques, the cost of wrought iron fell to less than half its previous price. Engineers who had begun to use cast iron for many things now began to find new uses for wrought iron. The famous engineer Thomas Telford used wrought-iron chains for his great Menai suspension bridge, which was begun in 1819. It carried a continuation of the old Roman Watling Street to Anglesey as the new Holyhead Road. Wrought iron was used by the builders of the new railways for parts for their steam locomotives, for the tracks they ran on and for many of the bridges they had to cross. In the 1840s Isambard Kingdom Brunel used wrought iron plates for his steamship the *Great Britain*. Wrought iron was the supreme material of the Industrial Revolution until well after the middle of the nineteenth century.

The Coalbrookdale Company

In order to raise money to build a new furnace, in 1715 Abraham Darby mortgaged half the Coalbrookdale works to a banker in Bristol called Thomas Goldney. When Darby died in 1717 having made no will, his widow was left to sort out the future of the business, then valued at £4,200*. She divided the value of the business into shares of which Thomas Goldney received half for the loan he had made. Richard Ford, Darby's son-in-law, also bought shares in the company and, when Darby's widow died, shares were purchased in trust for her children. By 1718 the business was being generally referred to as the Dale or, less frequently, the Coalbrookdale Company. However, it was not until 1790 that the name Coalbrookdale Company was officially adopted.

*A pound (£) is equal to about U.S. $2.40 in today's money.

An engraving of the upper works at Coalbrookdale, made in 1758. The six horses are pulling a steam engine cylinder, made at the Coalbrookdale works. In the centre of the picture you can just see the square top of the blast furnace with smoke belching out of it; on the right, heaps of coal are being burnt to make coke to use in the blast furnace. On the far side of the furnace pool two horses are pulling a waggonway truck down towards the works. Behind them is Dale House where Abraham Darby II lived.

Abraham Darby's son, also called Abraham, was only six when his father died, so Richard Ford took over the management of the business. The firm's finances were controlled by Thomas Goldney. By 1729 Abraham Darby II, as he is usually known, was being trained in the company works and in 1738 he became Richard Ford's partner.

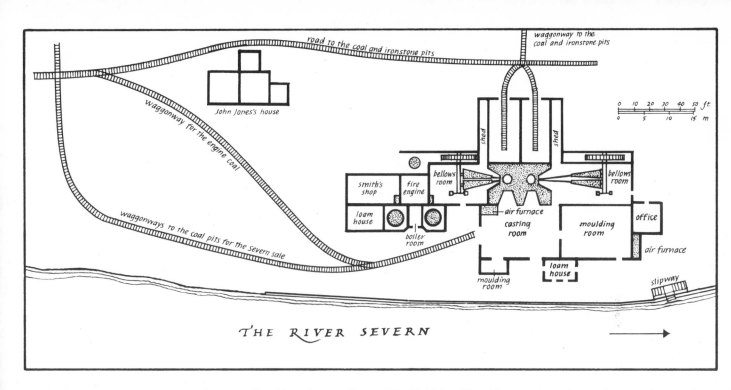

The Madeley Wood Ironworks, redrawn from a plan made in 1772. John Jones, whose house is shown on the plan, was a master collier and partner in the Madeley Wood company when it was set up in 1757. Abraham Darby III took over the ironworks in 1776.

Young Abraham was an experimenter like his father and by this time he knew a great deal about foundry work and blast furnaces. He had plenty of new ideas he wanted to try out and under his guidance the company continued to expand. One of his most successful achievements was setting up a new works with two blast furnaces for smelting pig iron. He built these on land he had leased at Horsehay Farm in the north of Dawley parish. Much work was needed to convert the old farm into a modern ironworks. An old millpond was greatly enlarged to make certain of enough water power to work the bellows. A steam pumping engine for returning the water to the pool once it had passed over the waterwheel was ordered from the Coalbrookdale works. Waggonways were built to carry raw materials to the furnaces at Horsehay and to carry iron to the River Severn and to the Coalbrookdale works. Darby leased mines at Horsehay which provided coal and iron ore for the new works, and took over agricultural land to supply food for his horses and timber for the new waggonways.

The first furnace at Horsehay began smelting in 1755. In 1756 the Seven Years War with the French began; the demand for iron therefore increased and the second Horsehay furnace was completed in the same year. Most of the pig iron smelted in the Horsehay furnaces was not used in Coalbrookdale but was taken to the Stour Valley in Worcestershire, or even into mid-Wales, where it was turned into wrought iron.

The company continued to expand its works in the second half of the eighteenth century, when the iron industry in Shropshire was generally very prosperous. By the 1780s, when Abraham Darby III, grandson of the first Abraham Darby, was a partner in the works, the company owned furnaces at Ketley, Madeley Wood and Donnington Wood, as well as at Coalbrookdale and Horsehay, and forges at Coalbrookdale and Bridgnorth. New Boulton and Watt engines began to replace the old Newcomen steam pumping engines

25

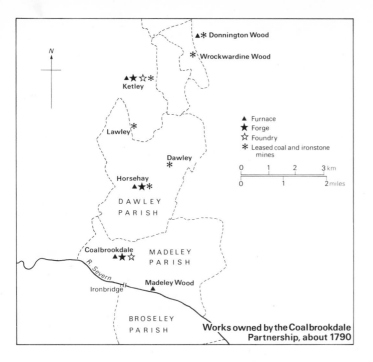

and the company continued to lease large areas of farmland and mining land. During Abraham Darby III's time the Coalbrookdale Company was probably one of the largest iron-making businesses in the country. The Darby family had slowly bought back all the shares held by Thomas Goldney's heirs and the company was now owned jointly by Richard Reynolds (son-in-law of Abraham Darby II) and the Darby family. By 1798, it was valued at £95,424.

Other industries

Meanwhile other industries were flourishing in the Severn Gorge area. Because there was plenty of cheap coal, lead ore was brought from Wales to be smelted. The pigs of lead were then shipped down the River Severn to Bristol which was the main centre of the lead trade.

Pottery was still being made in the village of Jackfield just downstream from the gorge. Most of the potteries seem to have been little more than family cottage industries making small numbers of mugs and dishes in coarse earthenware. But in the second half of the eighteenth century one family called

Thursfield began to make a special type of black earthenware decorated in gilt. Pieces of this Jackfield Ware (such as mugs, teapots and large jugs) were exported to America.

For many years very fine pottery, known as porcelain, had been imported into Europe from China. Gradually the European potters tried to make similar porcelain themselves. In the 1770s porcelain was made in Shropshire for the first time at Caughley, at the east end of the Severn Gorge. This was only about thirty years after porcelain was first made in London. By about 1800 two porcelain works had been started in the new village of Coalport at the lower end of the gorge. These were later to combine to form the Coalport Company.

In 1786 William Reynolds, a great grandson of Abraham Darby I, had a tunnel dug from near the river at Coalport towards some coalmines under Blists Hill about one kilometre (half a mile) away. He hoped to be able to move the coal from the pits without having to lift it up the mine shafts to the surface at Blists Hill only to lower it down to river level again. When the tunnel was only about 300 metres long, the workmen struck a spring of natural bitumen. This tar-like substance flowed out of the ground at a rate of about 4,000 litres (900 gallons) a week. A small industry grew up at the mouth of the tunnel to make some of the bitumen into a medicine thought to cure rheumatism, while the rest was sold as pitch for waterproofing ropes and the hulls of ships.

Also at Coalport there were several works making iron chains which were sold to the mine owners for use in the deep mine shafts which were becoming much more common. At the end of the eighteenth century there was a timber yard and a ropeworks there too; these survived for some years into the nineteenth century.

Coal which could not be made into coke was used to heat the kilns for firing bricks made out of local clay. The ironmasters used thousands of bricks a year, and many of them were special bricks which were used to line the inside of the blast

right: *Coalport, in the late eighteenth century, showing the bottle kilns where Coalport china was first made.*

above: *Some pieces of black Jackfield Ware, made in the second half of the eighteenth century.*

right: *Coalport fruit plates made between 1805 and 1810.*

furnaces. These had to be made to withstand the very great heat inside the furnaces. Bricks and roofing tiles were also needed for building houses. There was no difficulty in obtaining plenty of clay as this was found close to the seams of coal in the mines. As a result there were numerous brickworks and tileworks in the district by the 1770s.

As the amount of iron ore smelted in the district increased, more limestone for the blast furnaces was needed. Quarrying and mining limestone became another flourishing industry in several parts of the district. Some limestone was still burnt in kilns and the lime used for building and agriculture.

Many of the ironmasters seem to have leased farm land. This may have been for a number of reasons. Gone were the days when workpeople were paid in food, but the ironmaster who had agricultural land could provide food for his workforce and for his horses in years when it was in short supply.

There were other advantages for the men with land. If there was coal and ironstone beneath the surface, they could mine it themselves and so ensure a good supply for their ironworks. They could also cut down trees for timber, to build houses, and to use for the wooden beams of the steam pumping engines. If an ironmaster leased land he was able to build waggonways across it without having to pay other landowners for the right of way. His timber could also be used for the wooden tracks and for the waggons.

Mining of coal and ironstone was developing rapidly. The invention of the Newcomen engine gave miners a powerful pump which made it possible for them to work much deeper

pits. It also increased the demand for coal as fuel to fire the pumping-engine boilers at about the same time that ironmasters were buying more coal for use as coke.

A new method of mining coal had been pioneered in Shropshire in the seventeenth century. One constant problem of mining is the support of the roof while the mineral is being extracted. Originally miners drove narrow tunnels into the coal-face, leaving walls of coal, known as pillars, between each work-space. Conditions for the men were very bad as it was extremely difficult to get a flow of fresh air into the narrow tunnels. Later, when most of the coal had been extracted, the pillars were removed. This was highly dangerous as whole sections of roof could collapse. If, on the other hand, the pillars were not removed, large amounts of coal were left behind in the mine.

The new technique invented in Shropshire was called long-wall mining. By this method a long face of coal was mined by a number of miners working simultaneously, while the roof was supported first by wooden pit-props near the actual coal-face and later by artificial pillars or walls of rock and rubble. This method, as well as making it possible to extract more coal with less danger, made working conditions easier for the men as the long open face could be ventilated by air drawn right along it. Long-wall mining proved very successful and by the eighteenth century was the method used in most mines in Shropshire. It soon spread to other mining areas and is still used today, for the long open coal-face makes it possible for modern coal-cutting machinery to be used.

right: *This picture of Coalbrookdale from the south-west in 1758 shows how rural the area still was, despite all the industries. The longest row of cottages is Tea Kettle Row (see page 30).*

left: *Shovelling limestone and coal into a lime kiln was a dangerous occupation, but lime was important for fertilising the land. The sketch was made in 1804.*

far left: *Although brick-making used to be an important industry in the Severn Gorge area, the only remains of the industry now are old brick kilns like this one, crumbling and overgrown with creeper.*

Life in the gorge

In the days before steam-powered blowing engines were used, the ironmasters had to build their works close to streams with enough flow of water to turn their waterwheels. This often meant that the works were in very isolated places. So they also had to build homes for their workpeople. The Darby family, for example, built many rows of cottages in Coalbrookdale as well as near other works they owned.

As the company expanded they needed more men to run the new furnaces and ironworks and by the middle of the eighteenth century there was not enough local labour to meet their needs. Providing homes for workers, as well as offering high wages, as the Coalbrookdale Company did during the eighteenth century, were the best ways of attracting workers to the area.

Lured by the high wages, skilled workers, who were needed for some jobs in the blast furnaces and foundries, often came to the Severn Gorge district from other iron-making areas, particularly from the nearby Black Country. Unskilled workers, on the other hand, came to the ironworks from the rural parts of Shropshire, Staffordshire, and neighbouring Welsh counties. With the expansion of the east Shropshire coalfield, there was an increasing demand for unskilled workers here too. Some farmworkers also moved to the Severn Gorge area because agricultural wages there were higher than in rural areas with no industries. Often the farmworkers' children would find jobs in one of the local industries, while the fathers remained in agriculture. Many new workers came into industry in this way. There was also a noticeable migration of potters from Staffordshire to the Broseley area near the Severn Gorge. As we saw, the population of the east Shropshire coalfield in 1711 had been about 11,500. By the end of 1760 it had reached 20,000 and by 1801 it was over 34,800.

Work for the men in the forges and blast furnaces was tough and hard. Many of the men were highly skilled and worked very long hours. Blast furnacemen worked twelve-hour shifts from six till six and they had to work seven days a week to keep the furnaces in continuous blast. On Sundays the shifts changed over so the men who had done the day shift had to do the night shift as well. This meant that on alternate Sundays

Comparative wages

1776

Farm-labourer in Broseley	board and 4s a week, 6s in the harvest
Foundry-worker in Coalbrookdale	8s – 10s 6d a week (often much more)
Collier	1s 8d a day – 18s 4d for 11 day fortnight

1796

Farm-labourer in Broseley	10s a week
Ironworker in Broseley	£1 10s – £2 a week
Farm-labourer in Madeley	9s a week, 10s in summer
Unskilled ironworker in Madeley	11s a week, 12s in summer
Skilled ironworker in Madeley	up to £2 a week

£ = pound (equal to about U.S. $2.40 in today's money)
s = shilling (There were 20 shillings to a pound.)
d = penny (There were 12 pennies to a shilling.)

the men worked twenty-four hours. Forge workers also worked a twelve-hour day. Puddling, especially, was very hard work and the working life of a puddler was said to be over by the time he reached forty.

Mining was well paid too but it was dangerous as well as very tiring. Some miners worked twelve-hour shifts and others only six- or eight-hour shifts. Although long-wall mining was safer than the old methods there were still frequent accidents and the health of most miners was permanently damaged by the time they were fifty because of the damp and bad air in the mines.

The cottages which the Darby family built for their workers were similar to those built by other ironmasters but compared very favourably with the cottages of agricultural labourers in other parts of Shropshire. They usually had two rooms on the ground floor and two bedrooms above. The row of cottages in the photograph, known as Tea Kettle Row, was one of the earliest groups of cottages built by the company in about 1753. Of course not all people employed in the Darby works lived in company cottages and some workers did not even live in the villages where they worked. Instead they walked to work, often several kilometres, from nearby towns.

below: *A blacksmith's forge in 1802. The long lever was used for working the bellows and the crane for heavy lifting work.*

bottom: *Tea Kettle Row.*

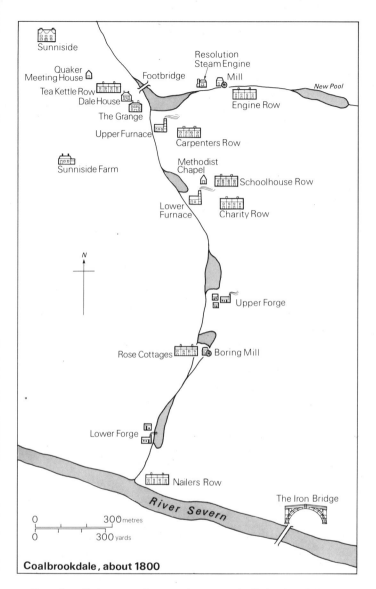

Coalbrookdale, about 1800

Despite all the extra homes that were built in the eighteenth century, there was still a shortage in east Shropshire owing to the sudden increase in population. For instance, in January 1782 the population of Madeley parish (which included Coalbrookdale, Ironbridge, Coalport, Blists Hill, Madeley Wood and Madeley Court) was 2,690 and there were only 440 houses (an average of 6 people per house). By March 1801 the

overcrowding had eased slightly: although the population had nearly doubled to 4,758, there were now 943 houses in the parish (an average of 5 people per house).

Providing homes for their workpeople may have been a necessity for ironmasters in Shropshire but many of them also tried to look after the general wellbeing of their employees and their families. The Darby family were unique in Shropshire for the number of facilities they provided for their workers. They built schools, and provided company shops and cottages for widows. Charity Row in Coalbrookdale is one such group of cottages built by the Darbys to house the widows of company employees. While Abraham Darby III (page 25) was running the works, the company began paying yearly rent for a mill where the workers and their families could grind their own grain free of charge.

It was a member of the Darby family – Abraham Darby II's widow, Abiah – who first suggested founding Sunday schools in east Shropshire. Sunday schools already existed in Gloucestershire and Yorkshire and in 1784 Abiah wrote to John Fletcher, the vicar of Madeley, pressing him to start similar schools in Shropshire 'for the benefit of poor children who have and are suffered to play and riot about on that day, which is and ought to be dedicated to Divine worship'. At a time when most children started work before the age of ten, the only chance they had of receiving any education was at Sunday school. Reading and writing, as well as the principles of good moral behaviour, were taught to children who were working six days a week.

The Darbys themselves lived near their work. Just before he died in 1717, Abraham Darby I had arranged to have a new house built. This was probably the house now called the Grange (or Rosehill House), near Tea Kettle Row and between the Upper Furnace and the Quaker Meeting House. His son, Abraham Darby II, lived at Dale House, next to the Grange until he built himself a new house called Sunniside, in

left: *The Grange, Coalbrookdale.*

right: *The Old Row, Horsehay. Cottages built in the mid-eighteenth century by the Darby family.*

about 1750. This house had ornamental gardens and was situated on the west side of the dale. If you look carefully at the engraving on page 29 you can just see the house and grounds on top of the hill. Sunniside was demolished in the nineteenth century.

As business prospered throughout the eighteenth century, the Darbys began to enjoy an increasingly comfortable life. We still have some of Abraham Darby III's house accounts which give us some idea of the family's standard of living at this time. Supplies of wine, cider, chocolate and cocoa were regularly ordered. The family bought copies of a variety of newspapers and magazines. Darby himself bought clothes – hats, shoes and stockings are recorded – on visits to London and in 1777 he bought a wig. In 1776, when many improvements were made to the house, Darby bought new carpets and various items of silver, pewter and glass.

Although by this time the village of Coalbrookdale had become a settled and thriving community with a population of skilled workers employed in a variety of crafts, the story in some other parts of the gorge was not the same. Places like Caughley, and tile- and brick-making areas such as Jackfield remained small isolated settlements. Other villages grew up solely to serve the new ironworks and coalmines in the district. Unlike what was happening in other parts of England there

was no sign that any large town containing many different industries might develop in the gorge area.

The new villages, especially those on the coalfield, were built very close to the mines and would often consist of no more than blocks of company cottages without even a chapel, shop or public house. The people who came to live in them must have been very isolated since transport in the gorge was still very difficult. The Horsehay works and cottages, for example, had been built in a remote part of Dawley parish far from the nearest established village and, similarly, the Donnington Wood furnaces were about 5 km (3 miles) away from the nearest church. People did of course manage to get to the towns on occasions; coalminers from the area are said to have made regular journeys to nearby towns on Reckoning Mondays – two days after they received their fortnightly pay – to frequent the public houses there.

But for most villagers in the eighteenth and early nineteenth centuries before the great revolution in transport, their village and not the town was still the focus of social life. Many people living in these small outposts must have heard very little about what was going on in the rest of the country. Even so, this may have been better than living in one of the industrial towns that were beginning to grow in other parts of Britain.

6 Transport

Iron on the waggonways

Although the wooden waggonways had been used for many years by the coalmine owners, it was apparently not until about 1740 that they were used by any of the ironmasters. At about that time the Coalbrookdale Company built waggonways for their own use. Much earlier than this the company had been supplying cast-iron wheels for waggons to run on several coalmine waggonways. These proved very much more hard wearing than wooden wheels. But there was one disadvantage: the iron wheels tended to wear away the wooden rails, which meant that new track had to be laid fairly frequently. To minimise this laborious and time-consuming task many waggonway owners laid a strip of wood on top of the track to take most of the wear; this could be replaced comparatively easily. In 1767 the Coalbrookdale Company pioneered a completely new idea when they replaced this wooden strip by a strip of iron. This of course did not wear out so quickly, and before long many waggonway owners were copying the idea. But it was to be another twenty years before rails made completely of iron were used anywhere.

The use of waggonways spread throughout the area. In 1785 one of the partners of the Coalbrookdale Company claimed that they owned over 32 km (20 miles) of track. Of course this was not open to the public. The waggonways were built by industrialists to carry their own goods. There were no engines to pull the waggons along; the waggons normally ran downhill to the river under their own weight and the empty waggons were dragged up again by horses.

The wheels of the waggons used on the waggonways all had a flange on one side to prevent them from slipping off the rails. This flange made it impossible for the waggons to be used on ordinary roads as the flange would either break off or cut into the road. A man named John Curr realised that a system of track which did not require flanged wheels might have great

above: *Waggonway trucks once used in the Ironbridge area.*

left: *An iron wheel on some flanged plateway track at the Ironbridge Gorge Museum.*

advantages. So he designed rails which incorporated the flanges on the rails rather than on the wheels. He called these plateways.

The system was very popular for a number of years and many kilometres of plateway track were laid in the Severn Gorge area. But, later, steam locomotives were built with flanged wheels on raised track and so the plateways gradually ceased to be used.

Boats on the Severn

Towards the end of the eighteenth century people tried to make it easier for boats to travel up the River Severn by building towpaths. In 1796 William Reynolds (page 26) had a towpath built through the Severn Gorge at his own expense. Gradually over the next ten years other men arranged for more towpaths to be built until the whole stretch from below Gloucester to Shrewsbury was completed. Most boats were pulled up-river from below Gloucester by horses – often two horses to a boat. But even as late as 1850 a few men in the gorge were still employed to haul boats along in gangs.

All goods such as fish, wine, stone, iron, coal and wood were

carried by water and even people wishing to travel from one town to another would go by boat. As well as the traffic up and down the river, many boats would be crossing from one bank to another, especially in the area of the Severn Gorge where there was no bridge.

The Iron Bridge

The River Severn frequently floods and crossing by ferry could often be very hazardous. But many of the ironmasters had to get raw materials from across the river. The Coalbrookdale Company had to ferry limestone across, as well as many of its workpeople. In the late 1770s two bridges were built in the gorge. The first to be opened was called the Wooden Bridge. It seems almost certain that quite substantial parts of this bridge were made of iron although the roadway was of wood and the pier in the middle of the river was made of stone. Unfortunately this bridge was pulled down in the late eighteenth century and only the abutments of the original structure remain.

The second bridge to be opened was a very much more impressive structure. Because of the steep banks of the gorge it was decided to build a single-span bridge springing from high abutments. Among the people involved in the bridge-building project were John Wilkinson and Abraham Darby III.

At first the people who were financing the bridge discussed the idea of building it of iron. But it looks as if they became a little frightened of this idea because in May 1776 they advertised for someone willing to build a single-span bridge either of stone, brick or timber. It seems that no one answered their advertisement because a month later the committee had agreed to build a bridge completely of iron. It is probable that the final shape of the bridge was the responsibility of Abraham Darby III, who agreed to cast the pieces for the bridge and to be in charge of erecting it.

The bridge is made up of five separate ribs which cross the river in one single span. These were each cast in two pieces which, when the bridge was erected, were lowered into position until the crown of the arch met over the river. A level roadway of thick iron plates was then laid across the river supported by these arches.

left: *Animals had to be walked to market. If there was no bridge they had to be ferried over the rivers or made to swim across. Even flat boats could overturn if the animals were frightened.*

right: *An early nineteenth-century Coalport china jug with a picture of the Iron Bridge painted on it.*

When the Iron Bridge was built not a single screw, nail or rivet was used. The men who designed the bridge had never handled large iron structures before and they had to find their own techniques. The joints they used were those which a carpenter making a wooden bridge or a piece of wooden furniture would have used. But what they built has lasted for nearly two centuries, though between 1973 and 1975 it had to be repaired. These repairs were not due to bad workmanship on the part of the builders; they were necessary because the bridge abutments had begun to slip towards the river because the sides of the gorge are very unstable.

When we look at the bridge today it is easy to understand why it caused so much interest, and why the little town which sprang up in that part of the gorge took its name from the bridge. The single span arch high over the river is beautiful, and the use of iron in this way was unique. Compared with the heavy stone structures being built at that time, it looks incredibly light and elegant. Many artists visited the Severn Gorge to make paintings of the bridge. But, despite the universal interest in the Iron Bridge, no one else tried to erect similar bridges for over ten years.

This picture of the Iron Bridge was taken in 1975 when work was being carried out to save the bridge from being broken as the abutments slipped towards the river. The roadway is held up by five arches which are cross-braced in several places to make the structure more rigid.

right: The date 1779 on the railings of the Iron Bridge was probably the year the castings were made. To erect and finish the bridge took two more years.

far right: Carpenters' joints used to fasten pieces of iron together. On the right is a 'dovetail' joint and in the centre a 'through tenon' joint with wedges.

Heavy stage waggons were used to carry goods all over England in the eighteenth and early nineteenth centuries.

This toll house was built by Thomas Telford when he was rebuilding Watling Street (now the A5). In 1973 the road was widened, the toll house was taken down very carefully and re-erected at Blist's Hill in the Ironbridge Gorge.

In February 1797, sixteen years after the bridge was opened, and eighteen years after the arches were put in place, all but one of the bridges over the River Severn were damaged by a very severe flood. The one bridge which escaped was the new Iron Bridge. Placed as it was high above the water, with no piers to be undermined or washed away by the flood, the Iron Bridge now showed its worth. Within a few months the great engineer, Thomas Telford, had replaced the old stone bridge at Buildwas, at the head of the Severn Gorge, with an iron bridge cast by the Coalbrookdale Company. Many more orders were to follow, and very soon other engineers were beginning to build cast-iron bridges. By the mid-Victorian period most of the new bridges built in Britain were made of iron.

Roads and canals

While the Iron Bridge was being constructed, work had also taken place on new roads to connect it with existing routes. Road transport was still not good, though many improvements had been made during the previous fifty years. In 1725 part of Watling Street had been put in the care of a turnpike trust, a company which was allowed to charge tolls to raise money to improve the road. Several other roads in the area were also turnpiked but it was still easier to send heavy goods by water. A horse can pull a much heavier load on water than on land.

But the River Severn – useful as it was for carrying heavy goods – only ran south to the Bristol Channel or north to Shrewsbury and Wales. The Duke of Bridgewater built the first British canal of modern times from his coalmines near Worsley to Manchester in 1761. Very shortly after this his brother-in-law, Earl Gower, who owned mines near the Severn Gorge, had a canal built on his own land to carry coal.

During the next twenty years a network of canals was built in the Midlands. The most important of these for the people of the Severn Gorge was the Staffordshire and Worcestershire Canal which joined the River Severn at a point about 32 km (20 miles) south of the Severn Gorge. This place soon became known as Stourport. The new canal made it much easier for heavy goods to be moved to the Midlands, the potteries, and even to Liverpool and Manchester.

The records of the Coalbrookdale Company show that many shipments of goods were sent down the River Severn to be transferred to canal narrow boats at Stourport. Before the canal was built, there was only one house at this part of the river. But as more and more traffic began to use the basin, a small town grew up – a new town entirely stimulated by the canal.

left: *An engraving of the small village of Stourport made only a few years after the Staffordshire and Worcestershire canal was opened in 1772*

below: *Small iron tub boats were used for transporting goods on all the canals in the Ironbridge area.*

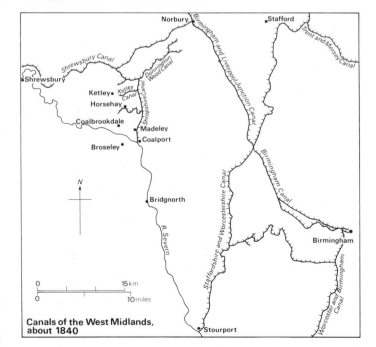

Canals of the West Midlands, about 1840

The Shropshire ironmasters soon began to build their own canals. They then realised that they needed a way of transferring their boats from the canal they had built on the high land above the gorge down to the river level. To have built flights of locks would have been extremely expensive and the time taken to work boats through the locks would have been so great as to render the whole canal virtually useless. The problem was solved by using very small iron boats which were floated onto little trucks and winched out of the water at the

above: *Part of the track of the inclined plane built between the canal on the high land and the Coalport canal below. It had been overgrown for many years but in 1975 new rails were laid to restore it to its original condition.*

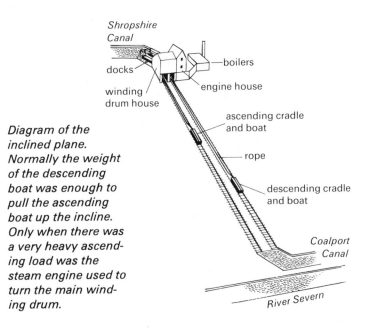

Diagram of the inclined plane. Normally the weight of the descending boat was enough to pull the ascending boat up the incline. Only when there was a very heavy ascending load was the steam engine used to turn the main winding drum.

Labels in diagram:
Shropshire Canal
docks
boilers
winding drum house
engine house
ascending cradle and boat
rope
descending cradle and boat
Coalport Canal
River Severn

end of the high canal. They were then lowered down tracks similar to a railway and allowed to run into the lower canal where they floated off the trucks again.

One of these tracks, which were called inclined planes, ended in a short length of canal close to the River Severn at Coalport (page 26). When the canal was built in 1792, there was no village. William Reynolds (page 26) built wharves and a very large warehouse so that goods could be transferred from the canal to the river. He encouraged men to build their works there in the hope of building up an industrial community. The name Coalport probably started almost as a joke because of the large amount of coal which travelled down the incline. But, despite Reynolds' efforts, Coalport did not grow into a thriving town as Stourport had done.

The first locomotives

Another step forward in transport also took place at Coalbrookdale. In 1802 a young man named Richard Trevithick visited the works. He was the son of a mine engineer from Cornwall and had spent most of his early years working with steam pumping engines. In 1797, at the age of twenty-six, he had begun to experiment with high-pressure steam engines. James Watt had always refused to use high-pressure steam as he considered it too dangerous but Trevithick realised that by using steam at a high pressure he could make a much lighter engine than the low-pressure Watt engines. By reducing the weight, Trevithick made it possible to mount a steam engine on wheels. He was not, however, the first man to experiment with the idea of steam locomotion. William Murdock, an engineer employed by James Watt, had made a model steam locomotive in 1786, and a Frenchman named Cugnot built two full-sized steam locomotives in 1769 and 1770, but neither of these men had carried on with his experiments.

In 1801 Trevithick built a steam locomotive which he tested

An engraving by Rowlandson of 'Catch me who can', the locomotive that Richard Trevithick took to London in 1808. Passengers were taken for rides at a shilling a time. The carriage is exactly like a road coach.

near his home at Camborne. Unfortunately while it was left unattended the boiler ran dry and the whole engine was destroyed by fire. During the next year Trevithick went to Coalbrookdale to carry out more experiments with high pressure steam. Parts worth £246 – a large amount of money in those days – were made for him by the Coalbrookdale Company for an experimental high pressure engine. The company also built a steam locomotive to Trevithick's design to be used on their waggonways. During his stay at Coalbrookdale, Trevithick also experimented with using steam to power a boat. Hearing that a steam engine for a mill in Macclesfield was to start its journey by barge, Trevithick obtained permission to connect the engine to two paddle wheels, one on each side of the barge. He later reported that the barge was able to travel at 11 kilometres (7 miles) an hour. Trevithick went on to design a steam engine for a small sailing vessel which was made for him by Matthew Murray of Leeds. William Reynolds had been very interested in the work Trevithick was doing. It may possibly have been the death of Reynolds in 1803 which brought the experiments at Coalbrookdale to an end.

Trevithick later built a steam locomotive which he displayed in London in 1808. Although many people went to see it and

the brave ones even risked riding behind it, he was bitterly disappointed by the lack of interest from other engineers and businessmen, so he abandoned his idea of a steam locomotive and turned his attention to other forms of engineering.

But Trevithick had given up too soon. Within a very few years, mine owners in the north-east of England were asking their engineers to build steam locomotives to use on their waggonways. The Napoleonic wars had caused a big rise in the price of animal food, but the mine owners had plenty of coal to feed the new 'iron horses'. Before building his London locomotive, Trevithick had designed one for the Wylam Colliery in Northumberland. But this locomotive was never used at the colliery; when the owner saw it he realised that his wooden waggonways were not strong enough to carry it, so the locomotive was taken off its wheels and used as a blowing engine in a Gateshead foundry. However, when Trevithick demonstrated his locomotive it must have had a profound effect on the engine men of the area.

In 1812 Matthew Murray built a steam locomotive to pull coal trains on Middleton Colliery railway, using the knowledge he had gained by building the steam-boat engine for Richard Trevithick. He paid Trevithick £50 for the use of his design. About a year later William Hedley built the famous locomotive Puffing Billy to use on the railway at Wylam Colliery for which Trevithick's Northumberland locomotive had been designed. Over the next few years, at nearby Killingworth Colliery, George Stephenson built a number of locomotives to haul coal waggons on the colliery railway.

From building these waggonway iron horses Stephenson developed the idea and the necessary experience for building a passenger railway. His Stockton and Darlington Railway opened in 1825, and the Liverpool and Manchester Railway opened five years later. By the time Trevithick returned after a long stay in South America, George Stephenson had become a famous railway engineer and the railway age had begun.

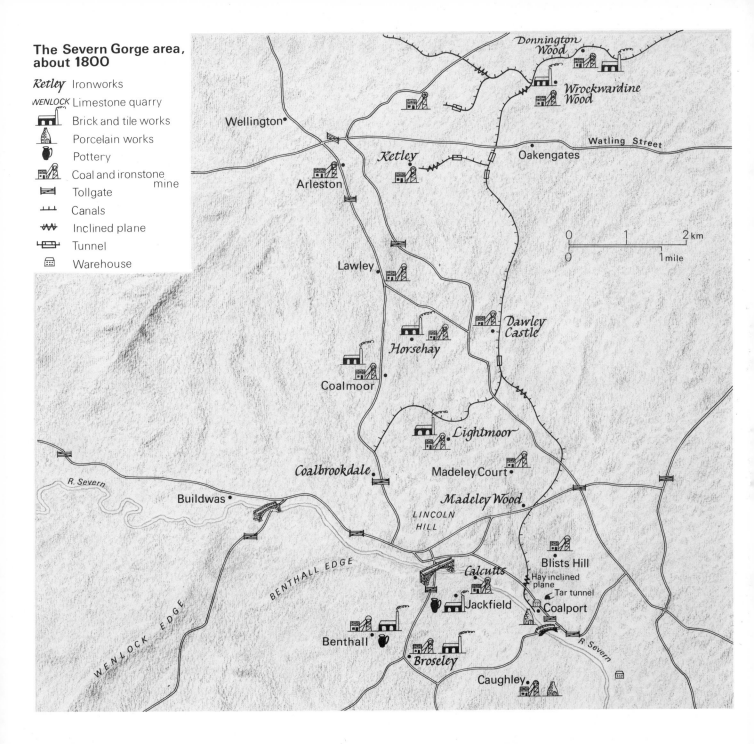

The Severn Gorge area, about 1800

Ketley Ironworks
WENLOCK Limestone quarry
Brick and tile works
Porcelain works
Pottery
Coal and ironstone mine
Tollgate
Canals
Inclined plane
Tunnel
Warehouse

Donnington Wood
Wrockwardine Wood
Watling Street
Wellington
Ketley
Oakengates
Arleston
Lawley
Dawley Castle
Horsehay
Coalmoor
Lightmoor
Coalbrookdale
Madeley Court
R. Severn
Buildwas
Madeley Wood
LINCOLN HILL
Blists Hill
BENTHALL EDGE
Calcutts
Hay inclined plane
Tar tunnel
Jackfield
Coalport
WENLOCK EDGE
Benthall
R. Severn
Broseley
Caughley

0   1   2 km
0   1 mile

7 Coalbrookdale and the New Iron Age

Prosperity and decline

During the whole of the eighteenth century and the first few years of the nineteenth century, the area around the Severn Gorge was a thriving, busy industrial community. Throughout this time, the iron industry was the most important factor in the livelihood of the people. Many of the smaller industries, and even the coalmines, were only successful because of the many ironworks in the district.

So many new ideas were put into practice in Coalbrookdale and the Severn Gorge that many famous British engineers visited the Ironbridge area. Even men from Germany, France, Italy, Sweden and America visited the district and many of them returned home to write accounts of what they had seen.

One Swedish engineer, called Erik Svedenstierna, visited the area in 1802 and wrote a detailed description of his visit:

'All furnaces and rolling mills at the Daleworks are driven by the customary large steam engines, but the turning and grinding machines are operated by the water of a small brook which winds down the valley. Further down the valley from the latter works and not far from the iron bridge there was a machine for boring cylindrical bellows, and a forge hammer constructed just as in our country, both of which were driven by water . . .

'When the forgeman was instructed to show me the process of flattening with the aid of such a hammer, as these are very rare in England, he raised the guard too soon so that the hammer hit the anvil itself 7 or 8 times before the piece of iron was in place. I could only imagine that the hammer and anvil would be ruined as a result but the smith assured me that this was a common occurrence and that the equipment was never damaged. I am mentioning this here in order to illustrate how these people have mastered the art of giving cast iron any required characteristic.

'In the neighbourhood there was also a porcelain factory [the Coalport China factory] which, however, I could not inspect. Nevertheless I saw teacups made here which come very near in whiteness to the best Paris porcelain and which had a more beautiful gilding than I had seen before in England. The English are also only just really starting to compete with the best porcelain factories.'

An Italian aristocrat who visited the gorge in 1787 described how astonishing and extraordinary a spectacle the activities in the gorge presented to a visitor at that time:

'The approach to Coalbrookdale appeared to be a veritable descent to the infernal regions. A dense column of smoke arose from the earth; volumes of steam were ejected from the fire engines; a blacker cloud issued from a tower in which was a forge; and smoke arose from a mountain of burning coals which burst out into turbid flame. In the midst of this gloom I descended towards the Severn, which runs slowly between two high mountains, and after leaving which passed under a bridge constructed entirely of iron. It appeared as a gate of mystery, and night already falling, added to the impressiveness of the scene.'

Arthur Young, the agricultural publicist, was also struck by the incongruity of Coalbrookdale's beautiful setting and its industrial activities, when he wrote, after a visit in 1776:

'Colebrook Dale . . . is a very romantic spot . . . Indeed too beautiful to be much in unison with that variety of horrors art has spread at the bottom: the noise of the forges, mills etc. with all their vast machinery the flames bursting from the furnaces with the burning of the coal and the smoak of the lime kilns, are altogether sublime.'

Travellers' descriptions like these can give us good pictures of what the area was like all those years ago, but we have to

J. M. W. Turner was among the famous people who visited Coalbrookdale. He painted this picture of the limeworks at Lincoln Hill (see the map on page 41) in 1797.

remember that what seemed to them enormous infernos of smoke and fire would make no such impression on later generations. The furnaces were still surrounded by a green landscape.

This period of prosperity and innovation in the Shropshire iron industry came to a fairly rapid halt at the end of the Napoleonic wars in 1815. Ironworks not only in Shropshire but in all parts of the country went through a period of acute depression as the demand for iron slumped. Many of the large companies had to reduce their output of iron and some smaller firms closed altogether. Even before the wars had ended one of the two blast furnaces at Coalbrookdale was blown out. A few years later, probably in 1818, the remaining blast furnace was blown out, leaving the famous works to make castings from pig iron brought from the company's other blast furnaces at Horsehay and Dawley Castle.

An English civil engineer, called Joshua Field, gave a very gloomy account of the works after his visit in 1821, during a tour through the Midlands:

'[I] walked through the dale works which are in a great measure deserted, the lease being nearly out, the Company are at little pains to keep them up. The Blast Furnaces are not worked and nothing is doing but some castings and a little bad mill work.'

The depression had hit Shropshire especially badly. Even by 1815, the wages paid by the ironmasters in the Severn Gorge district were lower than in other iron-making areas: wages in the Black Country at that time, for instance, were fifteen per cent higher than in Coalbrookdale. This trend was to continue through the century as other areas, like the Black Country, began producing iron in enormous quantities. Colliers and ironworkers in Coalbrookdale went on strike in 1820 and 1821 when the ironmasters threatened a reduction in wages

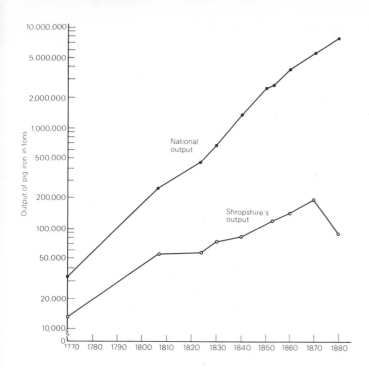

left: *The great warehouse at Coalbrookdale, built in the 1830s. It has cast-iron window sills and lintels. The cast-iron clock was added in 1843.*

far left: *Shropshire's share of the national output of pig iron between 1770 and 1880. The unusual scale used on the vertical axis makes it possible to plot very small and very large numbers on the same graph.*

because trade was so bad. In 1830, as the graph shows, Shropshire was still producing about ten percent of the British output of pig iron. In the next quarter of a century, when the iron industry was booming once more, the county's output doubled. But during this same period iron production in other parts of Britain increased far more, so that in 1869, its highest year of output ever, Shropshire produced less than four per cent of the national output.

The great increase in the production of iron in Britain was reflected in the many uses to which iron was now put. As well as its wide use in civil engineering, for such things as bridges and aqueducts, people soon began to use it in the building of factories, thus reducing the chances of disastrous fires which had caused great damage and loss of life in the past. Many small items of cast iron such as road markers, coalhole covers, and railings made during this period can still be seen in the streets today. Gone were the days when an iron cooking pot was such an important possession that it was mentioned in its owner's will and handed on from generation to generation. Even Iron Mad Wilkinson would not have complained about the variety of uses the Victorians made of his favourite metal.

In 1830 two young members of the Darby family had taken over responsibility for the works. They infused new life into it and by 1850 it was probably the largest iron foundry in the world. By 1851, the Company employed 3,500 people and was valued at £365,824. Francis Darby had decided to specialise in fine art castings, cast-iron furniture and house fittings such as spiral staircases, lamp brackets and door knockers.

In 1851 the Great Exhibition was held in the Crystal Palace in Hyde Park, London. The Coalbrookdale Company exhibited some very fine castings including a set of ornamental gates over 18 metres (60 feet) wide which spanned the entrance to the north transept. After the exhibition the gates were re-erected between Hyde Park and Kensington Gardens, where they can still be seen. Another exhibit was a statue of Andromeda, who, according to Greek mythology, was chained to a rock as a sacrifice to a sea monster. After the exhibition closed the statue was bought by Queen Victoria. These and various other exhibits sent by the Coalbrookdale Company caused great interest and spread the company's high reputation for fine art casting.

The Coalbrookdale Company sent a wide variety of wrought-iron wares to the Great Exhibition in 1851, including the famous pair of gates below.

A fine wrought-iron spiral staircase from the Coalbrookdale Company's catalogue.

A tile from a catalogue of the Maw company (about 1870).

A fruit plate shown by the Coalport Company at the Great Exhibition.

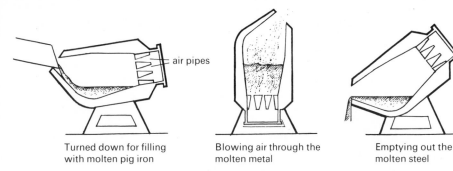

Turned down for filling with molten pig iron

Blowing air through the molten metal

Emptying out the molten steel

Bessemer's method for making steel is surprisingly simple: molten pig iron is poured into a giant 'jug' lined with firebrick. The jug is then placed upright and cold air blown into the iron through the pipes or tuyères. This causes a very violent reaction which showers sparks and molten metal high into the air. After about ten minutes the reaction ceases and the molten steel is ready to be poured out of the jug.

The Great Exhibition sparked off interest in art and design throughout the British Isles. It was perhaps this, as well as the long tradition of skilled work there, which led to the opening of a School of Art in Coalbrookdale. A new building to house it, together with the Coalbrookdale Literary and Scientific Institution, was built by the company in 1859. This was one more example of the company's continuing effort to provide as many facilities as it could for its workpeople.

By 1861, the population of Madeley parish had increased to 9,469, a reflection perhaps of the area's prosperity. However, after 1870, the Shropshire iron trade began once more to decline rapidly and this time there was no recovery. Between 1871 and 1891 over 1,000 people left Madeley parish.

The decline was partly due to the failure of the ironmasters to adopt new methods or to replace out-of-date equipment. It was also partly caused by a shortage of raw materials. Supplies of coal suitable for coking had run out, and there remained very little suitable limestone near at hand. There was still plenty of ironstone, although this had become difficult and expensive to mine, and it seems that some of the ironmasters found it easier to move the iron ore to the Black Country, where supplies of coal were available and where transport was easier, rather than smelt it in Shropshire. Competition increased from other parts of the country where deposits of iron ore had been recently found and which did not suffer the disadvantages of Coalbrookdale. Many ironworks in east Shropshire closed and there was increasing unemployment.

Some other industries in the gorge did continue to thrive, like the chinaworks at Coalport which was still flourishing towards the end of the nineteenth century. Maw and Company continued to make decorative tiles and in 1871 a new firm, Craven Dunhill, was manufacturing similar tiles at Jackfield.

A number of other new firms began making roof tiles in Jackfield and Broseley, using the good local clay. The brick-making industry also expanded. But these industries did not compensate for the large number of jobs lost as the iron trade in the area declined.

Cheap steel

A change in iron technology hastened the decline of the Shropshire iron industry still further. This was the new technique for making steel. Steel is a form of iron which men had known how to make for about three thousand years. It had been used for making swords, knives and springs. However, it could still only be produced in extremely small amounts. When, in 1856, Henry Bessemer showed how to make steel in large quantities, ironmasters in many parts of Britain began to use this new and relatively cheap method of production. Once large amounts of steel became readily available, engineers and machine-makers turned to this form of iron.

It was, of course, in the making of cast and wrought iron that the Ironbridge area had been important. Ironmasters in other parts of Britain quickly turned to making Bessemer steel. The men of Shropshire did not. There were several reasons for this. Because Shropshire had been one of the foremost iron-making districts for over a hundred years, it had a great amount of equipment which could still be used, which would be expensive to remove and replace, but which was becoming out of date.

As we saw, transport facilities in the gorge were not good compared with other iron-making counties and supplies of raw materials were deteriorating. Given these disadvantages, spending large amounts of capital buying equipment to make

The discovery of ores in the Cleveland hills in the early 1800s led to the founding of Middlesbrough. By 1881, the date of the picture, the town's output of pig iron had reached 2,676,000 tonnes and the population 56,000. Abundant local ore and coal and good transport facilities helped this rapid growth, advantages that were all lacking by then in Coalbrookdale.

Bessemer steel must have seemed a hopeless prospect to the ironmasters.

More ironworks in the area closed down and by 1883 the Coalbrookdale Company was no longer producing pig iron at any of its works. In the Dale castings were still being made, but all from pig iron bought from other companies. This still goes on. The works at Coalbrookdale have never closed. It is still a foundry, now making parts for cookers and fires, for engineering and the motor industry, though none of the iron that it uses is smelted in Shropshire.

Throughout the second half of the nineteenth century men left the Severn Gorge to look for work in other places. Many ironworkers and other skilled men went to the Black Country coalfield and others went to South Wales. Even by 1851 there were 1,800 migrants from Shropshire in Liverpool, Manchester and Bolton alone. Farmworkers also left Shropshire to go to the Black Country and the Birmingham area where wages were higher.

The River Severn ceased to be a commercial highway and by 1900 there were no barges using the river near Ironbridge. Grass began to cover the waste heaps, and old buildings began to crumble. The Coalport chinaworks closed in 1926 and by then the district was no longer an important industrial area. No new factories were being built on the old sites; instead, the early blast furnaces, the canals and the waggonways were left in the woods near the Severn Gorge and gradually the trees encircled them and hid them from view.

By 1951 the population of Madeley parish had declined to 8,059. The Craven Dunhill tileworks at Jackfield closed in 1952, and Maw and Company were taken over by a large tile company in Stoke-on-Trent and had ceased making tiles in Jackfield by the end of 1969. Although farming in this part of Shropshire had continued throughout the industrial expansion of the eighteenth and nineteenth centuries and parts of the area are still farmed today, industrial workers could not get jobs in farming as industry declined. Instead they had to leave the district to find jobs elsewhere.

In 1968, the area north of the gorge became part of Telford new town and many changes took place. Because the boundaries of the districts were then altered it is impossible to make exact comparisons of the size of the populations, but the development of the new town brought industries and prosperity to the area once more. By 1977 the population of the new Madeley and Ironbridge districts had increased to over 20,000. Two large new industrial estates were built in Madeley district employing over a third of the districts' population; engineering and manufacturing steel, aluminium and other metal goods were among the main industries. The new

An aerial view of the Severn Gorge at Ironbridge, looking east, taken in 1971 shows how rural the district has remained.

districts also became the home of many people commuting to work in the nearby big towns, such as Birmingham, or working in the power-station across the River Severn from Ironbridge. Many new houses, schools and shops were built in Madeley district to accommodate the large number of people coming from big industrial cities to live and work in this part of Shropshire.

A site of the Industrial Revolution

Only when industrial archaeologists in the 1970s began to search did the old sites in the Severn Gorge district come to light again. The decayed remains of the last two hundred years were carefully preserved in order to bring prosperity to the area once again as a new generation of tourists and travellers come to see the places where so many important techniques were given birth. The many industrial changes which were pioneered in the Ironbridge area had a profound and far-reaching influence on the whole of Britain and, later, the world. Iron changed from being an expensive, rather scarce metal, to one which was used for hundreds of different purposes.

The Ironbridge Gorge has been called the cradle of the Industrial Revolution. It is certainly true that the inventive genius of the men of the area sowed the seeds of the industrial society in which we live today. The Iron Bridge, still standing proudly over their river, is a fitting memorial to these great men.

Index

Acknowledgments

The author and publisher would like to thank the following for permission to reproduce illustrations:
front cover, pp. 11, 13, 14, 27 (above, below left), 28 (left), 29 Ironbridge Gorge Museum Trust; p. 4 Shropshire County Libraries Local Studies Department; pp. 5, 7 (above) Museum of London; pp. 6 (left), 10 (right), 19, 30 (below), 33, 36, 37 (right), 38 (below), 39, 44, 45 (centre right, below left) Arthur Vialls; pp. 6 (right), 12, 17, 20, 23, 37 (left), 40 Science Museum, London; pp. 7 (below), 24 British Library; p. 8 BBC Schools Publications; p. 9 Leonard Pole; p. 10 (left) Geffrye Museum; pp. 15, 28 (right), 30 (above), 35 (left), 45 (below right) Guildhall Library; p. 16 (above) M. T. Walters and Associates Ltd; p. 16 (below) Institution of Mechanical Engineers; p. 21 Trustees of the British Museum; p. 22 Peter Baker Photography; pp. 27 (below right), 35 (right) Geoffrey Godden of Worthing; p. 32 (left) Royal Commission on Historical Monuments; p. 32 (right) Barrie Trinder; p. 34 (above) Robert Harris; p. 34 (below) National Maritime Museum, London; p. 38 (above) British Waterways Museum; p. 43 Yale Center for British Art, Paul Mellon Collection; p. 45 (above) Illustrated London News; p. 47 Cleveland County Libraries; p. 48 Aerofilms; back cover Crown copyright, Science Museum, London

Much useful background information on Coalbrookdale and the Industrial Revolution in Shropshire can be found in Barrie Trinder's books:

The Darbys of Coalbrookdale, Phillimore 1974
The Industrial Revolution in Shropshire, Phillimore 1973
The Most Extraordinary District in the World, Phillimore 1977

The author and publisher are very grateful to Barrie Trinder for his help and advice in preparing this book.

front cover: *An engraving of the Iron Bridge over the River Severn by Michael Ellis, published in May 1782, after a painting by Michael Angelo Rooker.*

back cover: *Coalbrookdale at night painted by Philip de Loutherbourg in 1801.*

Drawings by Leslie Marshall
Maps by Reg Piggott

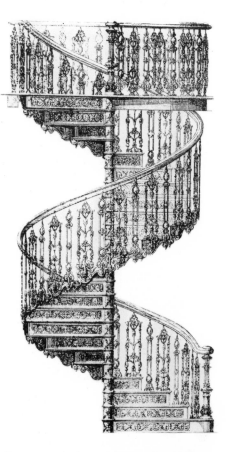

A fine wrought-iron spiral staircase from the Coalbrookdale Company's catalogue.

The Cambridge History Library

The Cambridge Introduction to History
Written by Trevor Cairns

PEOPLE BECOME CIVILIZED

THE ROMANS AND THEIR EMPIRE

BARBARIANS, CHRISTIANS, AND MUSLIMS

THE MIDDLE AGES

EUROPE AROUND THE WORLD

EUROPE AND THE WORLD

THE BIRTH OF MODERN EUROPE

THE OLD REGIME AND THE REVOLUTION

POWER FOR THE PEOPLE

The Cambridge Topic Books
General Editor Trevor Cairns

THE AMERICAN WAR OF INDEPENDENCE

BENIN: AN AFRICAN KINDGOM AND CULTURE

THE BUDDHA

BUILDING THE MEDIEVAL CATHEDRALS

CHRISTOPHER WREN
AND ST. PAUL'S CATHEDRAL

THE EARLIEST FARMERS AND THE FIRST CITIES

EARLY CHINA AND THE WALL

THE FIRST SHIPS AROUND THE WORLD

GANDHI AND THE STRUGGLE
FOR INDIA'S INDEPENDENCE

HERNAN CORTES: CONQUISTADOR IN MEXICO

THE INDUSTRIAL REVOLUTION BEGINS

LIFE IN A FIFTEENTH-CENTURY MONASTERY

LIFE IN A MEDIEVAL VILLAGE

LIFE IN THE IRON AGE

LIFE IN THE OLD STONE AGE

MARTIN LUTHER

MEIJI JAPAN

THE MURDER OF ARCHBISHOP THOMAS

MUSLIM SPAIN

THE NAVY THAT BEAT NAPOLEON

POMPEII

THE PYRAMIDS

THE ROMAN ARMY

THE ROMAN ENGINEERS

ST. PATRICK AND IRISH CHRISTIANITY

THE VIKING SHIPS

The Cambridge History Library will be expanded in the future to include additional volumes. Lerner Publications Company is pleased to participate in making this excellent series of books available to a wide audience of readers.

Lerner Publications Company
241 First Avenue North, Minneapolis, Minnesota 55401